un·ed·it·ed
/ˌənˈedədəd/
Healing Whispers

F.A. Khan

BookLeaf
Publishing
India | USA | UK

Presentation by *BookLeaf Publishing*

Web: www.bookleafpub.com

E-mail: info@bookleafpub.com

ISBN: 9789358317640

First edition 2023

To my parents,

for motivating me to start this journey;

To my husband,

for guiding me through it.

Acknowledgements

All my patients and their loved ones.

"Healing yourself is connected with healing others."
Yoko Ono

"Medicine, I said, begins with storytelling. Patients tell stories to describe illness; doctors tell stories to understand it. Science tells its own story to explain diseases."

Siddhartha Mukherjee;
The Emperor of Maladies

in·dex
/ˈin͵deks/

ageism
anaphylaxis
allergy
burnout
cataract
cadaver
coma
COVID-19
donor
family
identity
ingredient
memory
mind
pain
prayer
prayer 2
screening
surgery
soul
tumor
trauma
wristband
wellness

age·ism

/ˈāj͵iz(ə)m/

Geriatric:
WHO definition;
Older than 65 years of age.

Maternal:
American College of Obstetrics and
Gynecologists definition;
35 years of age.

Geriatrics is a medical specialty focused on elderly health services.

AMA: Advanced maternal age: one common definition is maternal age above 35.

anaphylaxis
/ ˌæn ə fə ˈlæk sɪs /

Peanut butter
Cream cake
Oatmeal cookies
Ice cream
Fish and chips
Alpha gal
Pollen and trees.

Last week flashes before my eyes
seconds to minutes
raspy breathing
dusky skin
panic in our eyes.

We walk down the picnic table and out onto the
lawn
clutching the backpack
Epipen and snack bag ready
safety in medicine.

Anaphylaxis: severe, life-threatening allergic reaction.

al·ler·gy
/ˈalərjē/

Time out.

Allergies to
Keflex
Penicillin
Latex
Fentanyl
Morphine
Strawberry
Dairy
Kiwi
Steroids

Her voice started out strong
eventually taking on a tone of despair
frustration

Is this list endless?

Does it even make sense?
Is she allergic to all of them?

I see the invisible thread of time
stretching out

taut
ready to snap while people wait to move on
does this list ever end?

What happens when you take any of these?
Who has an allergy to steroids? Kiwi?

Yes
I get hives and my brain feels like it is on fire.
They hear my words
see the pain in my eyes.

Agree
Agree
Agree

Everyone agrees;
Let's move onto the next checklist.

They don't see the scratches
the welts
that erupt and don't heal
they don't see the scars
my mind, my soul, my body;
A canvas
a testament tied to that red wristband.
Reconciled.

burn·out
/ˈbərnˌout/

60 seconds
60 minutes
24 hours
Weeks into months
365 days
Medical school
Residency training
Specialization;

Clinic
night shifts
late nights
early mornings
charting
accolades
felicitations
recognition
conferences
awards;

Years gone by
years ahead
days missed and moments lost
lives saved

sleepless nights
the line blurs.

Take a moment;
sip your tea
exercise
take a nap
sleep at night
pause
reflect
choose

Take a big breath and step into the next day.

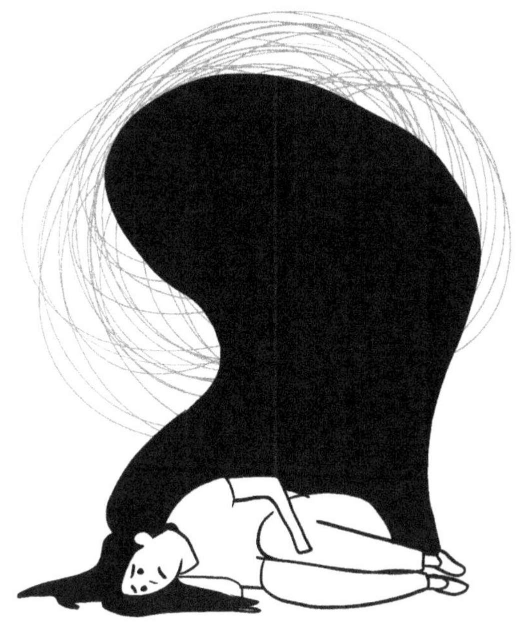

Burnout: more than half of US physicians report at least one symptom of burnout; twice the rate of the general working population.

cat·a·ract
/ˈkadəˌrak(t)/

Derived from the Latin cataracta
Meaning "waterfall"

How apt;
we are born with eyes closed
that open to the wondrous vision of the world
blue skies and white clouds, love shining in our
parents' eyes
the thrill of newness reflecting in ours.

time passes and then they burn
     shine
glisten with tears
    laughter
then life pulls a curtain down with age
protection from the visions of a world that does
not seem
what it once was;
  unseeing
a blessing in disguise.

ca·dav·er
/kəˈdavər/

Day one
the bright lights burn my eyes
or is it the formalin;

Hands steady
I mark my domain;

Skin the thoracic wall
Reflect the pectoralis major muscles
Dissect the thoracic wall
Explore the contents of the thoracic cavity;

The dark abyss pulls me into it
My heart skips a beat.

Situs Inversus
The professor's voice from behind.

Situs inversus: a rare genetic condition in which organs in your chest and abdomen are reversed. The heart is on the right side.

co·ma

/ˈkōmə/

The day shift nurse comes in
I like her;
warm smile that reaches her voice
spring in her step, humming a peppy tube
smell of fresh coffee
cinnamon?

Hey there, sunshine!
Today we have a surgery planned
you will do great!
They are going to fix you.

The team comes for their rounds;
22-year-old female
MVC, POD#3 s/p exlap, splenectomy; ORIF R
femur and Tibia

Nonresponsive

Stable C6-7 tr process fx
Stable 3-6th R rib fx, 7-12 L rib fx
B/L mandible fx

Plan: ORIF L humerus today
Replacing Mg and K

15

Cr elevated, changed abx

Unable to reach family.

The doctor shines a light in my eyes
Reactive bilateral, he says; celebrating a win.

Pupillary light reflex of the eyes is used to assess the brain stem function.

COVID-19
/ ˈkoʊ vɪd naɪn ˌtin /

I am on the COVID airway response team

Hour 11:
Ready to run on the next page
empty corridors
silence
yet panic;

Time to intubate
time to prepare.
Hand wash
N95 masks
Goggles
protective face shield
protective clothing
double surgical gloves
disposable anti-leakage shoe covers;

Quiet room
no positive pressure ventilation
I pray for an easy airway
And get ready to inject the medicine;

Our eyes meet

scared
unsure
no hope
dimmed

"He can't speak English," the nurse says
"Good thing I can speak Hindi," I say.
His eyes crinkle and gently close as I reassure
him.

"Will I live?" He had asked.

During COVID-19, strict precautions had to be taken for every procedure. When the patient could not breathe, they were supported by a breathing tube; intubation is the process of placing the breathing tube in the patient's airway.

do·nor
/ˈdōnər/

We wait around patiently
scrubbed and ready to go;
eyes averted
hearts overwhelmed
prayers answered for many;

Heart
Lungs
Liver
Small bowel
Pancreas
Kidney

Quick and precise
Not a moment wasted.

A beating heart stills;
While many others take up the rhythm.

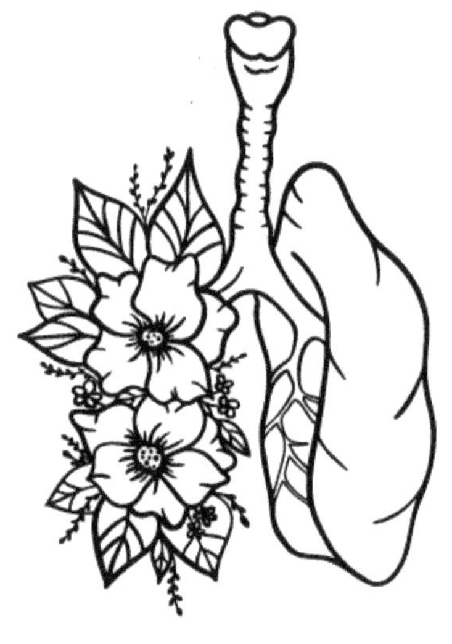

fam·i·ly
/ˈfam(ə)lē/

What does one say
when facing your child
not as her mother
but as her caregiver
The one she has put her faith in.

The MRI scans glow on the screen
magnified in the darkness of the room;
beckoning you close
yet taking you so far away
away into an abyss;
Her questioning eyes turn towards me.
Trusting
Questioning
I falter, take a deep breath, and reach across for
her hand.
Always in my hands.

i·den·ti·ty
/ī'den(t)ədē/

What's in a name?

Aptronym?
Euonym?

Dr. Hand
Dr. Chance
Dr. Quick
Dr. Foote
Dr. Assman
Dr. Knapp
Dr. Payne
Dr. Butt
Dr. Toothaker
Dr. Sleep
Dr. Kidd
Dr. Small
Dr. Bone
Dr. Strange
Dr. Graves
Dr. Gore
Dr. Burns

Blessed with a lifetime of service,
by choice or by fate?

in·gre·di·ent
/in ˈgrēdēənt /

Each day I write a new recipe;

Spices roast and aromas waft into my senses
My grandmother rolling out the dough
I sit next to her, cuddled into her warmth while
she bakes me bread.

Roasted chilies rubbed with spices
soaked in vinegar and steeped with love
the sun bakes us as we stretch out amongst the
platters of roasted tomatoes
the pickled vinegar jars twinkling in their home;
I smile as their juices flow onto the pages of my
recipe book
their memories staining the pages dark and
greasy.

I close my eyes and savor the flavors
East meets west;
I inherited my love for different cuisines from
my dad
Tacos, Pizza, and Biryani,
Skewered kababs and heartwarming bowls of
Pho.

I am frantic
writing fast
trying to hold onto memories and flavors
not much time remains;

Dry heaves and nausea pass over me in a wave

waves

no one said chemo was easy on the stomach.

mem·o·ry
/ˈmem(ə)rē/

Head,
shoulders knees and
Toes knees and
toes;

Wallet, glasses
Keys and phone
Keys and phone.

The mind plays tricks
strong and agile
muscle memory so strong
enabling tasks as mundane as driving home after
a sleepless night
surfacing effortlessly when thrown into deep
waters
rising above the murkiness that threatens to
drown;

Throwing a stitch
tightening the cord
stopping the blood flow
ebbing it to a trickle
while the clock ticked on;

Children raised
students taught
lessons learned and shared;

Yet, here I stand
straight and tall
strong
yet weak;

As memories struggle
shimmers of what once was
a figment, a story, a lifetime
unable to rise above the waters of my mind.

mind
/mīnd/

Shapeshifters
imaginary friends
buddies
self lives;

The mind splits
as it grapples the existence
of so many entities
Identities;

Nesting dolls.

Baby Emma
The angel;

Lorna
The silent one;

Wrigley
Wiley in her ways;

Sam
Calm and serene
yet cold and immutable;

Rayna
Seeking answers
and solace;

Shawn
Lost amongst the girls.

Dissociative Identity Disorder: having two or more separate identities.

pain
/pān/

Where does it hurt?
What does it feel like?
When did it start?
What makes it worse?
What lessens the pain?
What medications do you take at home?

aching
burning
sharp
stabbing
deep
visceral
superficial

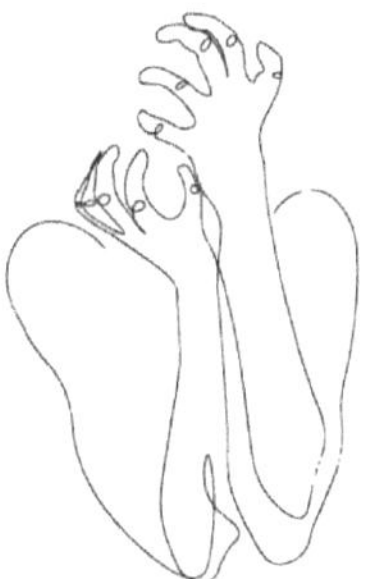

On a scale of one to ten, how bad is it?

I debate
What do I want to be seen as today?

drug seeking
        or opioid naïve?

prayer
/prer/

Ready to go, I ask?

Wait,
we want to say a prayer
Join us, they extend a hand;

I hold hands
as we circle her around the bed
heads bowed and eyes closed;
Asking for his love
His mercy
His strength
His blessing on her doctors;
That they have faith
and do not err.

Ameen,
Says my heart.
Do not hold my religious belief against her faith.
Let our prayers unite.

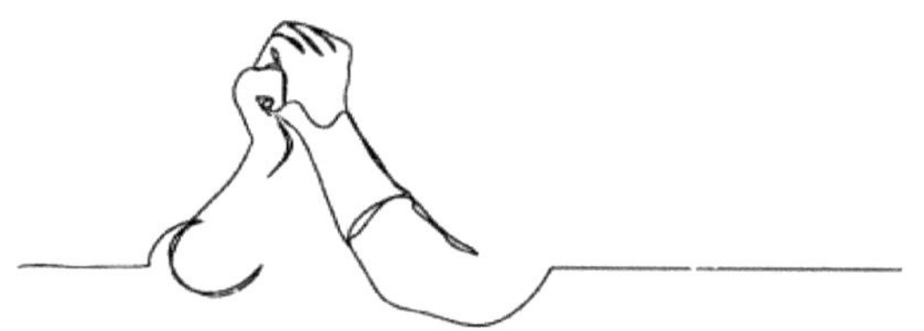

prayer²
/prer/

Ready to go, I ask?

Wait, we want to say a prayer
Join us, they extend a hand;

I hold hands
as we circle her around the bed
heads bowed and eyes closed;
Asking for his love
His mercy
His strength
His blessing on her doctors;
That they have faith
and do not err.

Amen,
Says my atheist heart.
Do not hold my lack of belief against her faith.

screen·ing
/ˈskrēniNG/

Breast cancer
Colonoscopy
Lung cancer
Osteoporosis
Prostate cancer
Lipids, blood sugar, routine labs.

The list is endless
Life after 40.

I turn and close my eyes
shedding my white coat for the patient's gown
shedding my armor
my entitlement of knowledge
the medicine burns through my veins and I enter
a blissful sleep
of uncertainty, awareness, mortality, and dreams.
Keep my secrets safe my friend.

sur·ger·y
/ˈsərj(ə)rē/

Scalpel;
Snip
Cut
Lance
Dissect
Incise.

Growth;
Swelling
Mole
Lesion
Growth
Lump
Tumor
Mass
Cancer.

A person
Reduced to a diagnosis;
Mitigate
Treat, cure
or limit?
Obliterate
Decimate?

soul
/sōl/

Lights ... Camera... Action

I stand frozen
or am I floating
a void encompasses me
yet I feel secure

beyond, I peer into the harsh lights that glow in
the center
of the room
I lay there
covered and draped
cut wide open
people scurry around

         loud

           it is so loud

alarms beeping and blaring
people shouting

Start CPR
  Epinephrine
   How many Epi's given?
    Did anyone run an ABG?
     Get an A line

My chest hurts

I see him pushing against my chest
I hear him counting in his head
  one Mississippi
   two Mississippi
    three Mississippi...

someone places another IV
yet another rushes off with a blood sample for
analysis
the machine hisses and pumps air into my lungs

   at least I am breathing, I think

Seconds tick away
Who is counting now... *one... two... three...*

  Countdown?

How long has it been?

  Is this me?

pink .. then pale.. then blue..

  Is this the end?

the world revolves around me

they want me back
they pray
they cry
they beg
some of them make a bargain with God
This is surreal

I feel wanted
loved
I feel the need to return
to belong

to not disappoint

Beep .. Beep.. Beep ..

a sound breaks across the chaos of the room
Hands pause and moments still

All eyes on the monitor.

CPR: cardiopulmonary resuscitation; the act of using chest compressions and mouth to mouth breathing to revive the patient.

tu·mor

——

/ˈtoomər/

I am more than the tremor in my hand
the visions and the sounds
the fumble and the fall.

I am more than the yellow color of my skin
the bile sludge
the firm mass
the trending markers
that refuse to dip.

I am more than the pulsating mass
that gathers all the blood
ready to spill
and flood me to death.

I am more than the beauty of my breasts
the firm mass
hidden and obscure
missed by all
until the screening was done.

I am more than the mole on my back
the many beauty spots
that refuse to fade

and take hold of more
than just my skin.

I am more than the tremor
the fall or the fumble
the tick of the clock;
I have nerves of steel
passion in my soul
faith to hold me strong
hope in my eyes and strength in my spine.

I hold on.

trau·ma
/ˈtrômə/

It is the irony of life
that a bullet lodged in my spine
damaged me beyond repair;

T4, they say
Paraplegia;
paralysis of my legs
can't move
can't walk
can't live, really live;

> *yet I breathe*
> *think*
> *dream*

Night comes and I close my eyes
let someone else bathe and clean me
rearrange my limbs
massage them into compliance
submission
cover me gently
kiss my brow
sweet dreams they say;

I close my eyes and see the grave

my friend

The bullet that lodged in my spine
had a twin that took his heart.

Wristband
/ˈris(t)ˌband/

Sometimes I feel I am a number.
An identity band
An appointment time in the scheduling book.

my disease defines me

I know not how I got it
how it entered my being
spread into my blood.

it courses in my veins
invades every organ I own

Some days, I feel fine
I wake up to a fresh morning
go for my follow up visit
her warm smile greets me and I feel a strength
inside.

Some days I can barely wake up
eyes heavy
limbs slumbering
energy sapped
my soul dry

maybe it will all be fine;
my day will go on, my life will go on.

Scan my name into your appointment book
Look at me
Let it register that I am more than a number

     a name
      a person
       an identity.

<h1 align="center">*well·ness*
/ˈwel-nəs/</h1>

Affirmation cards
Backpack
Coffee
Commemoration pin
Desk accessories
Earbuds
Flask
Framed photograph
Gift card
Hope and hugs
Ink pen or stylus
Jacket
Keurig
Lunch
Lab coat
Mug
Mask, personalized
Notes
Oil diffuser
Pen or plaque
Quick dry towel
Rubik's cube
Snacks
Scrub hat, *personalized*

Tote bag
Thank you email
Umbrella
Vacation
Water bottle
Xmas cookie
Yoga mat
Yeti
Zen calendar.

A Day off
Empathy
Meal train
Laundry service
Take your kid to school day
Lunch with my kids
Spa day
Charts done, patients seen, lives saved
Time given
*   yet gained*
Satisfaction.

Happy Doctors' Day.

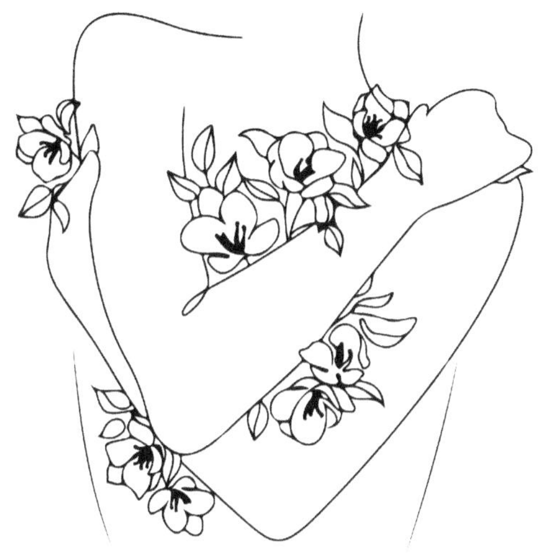

Physician wellness (well-being) is recognized for its intrinsic importance and impact on patient care.

About the author

Dr. F.A. Khan is an immigrant physician. She was born in India and moved to the United States for higher studies. She now lives there with her family.

She loves to read and spends her time exploring different places and connecting with people. Her writing explores stories about relationships and issues that deal with diversity and connections between different people.

She has a passion for reading and has rekindled her love for creative writing. After completing the Columbia Narrative Medicine Workshop and the facilitator training at the Northwest Narrative Medicine Collaborative, she uses narrative medicine skills to connect with patients beyond the hospital visit.

Dr. Khan has a vision to heal with words and has published some of her writings on kevinmd.com. She is currently working on a compilation of stories; this is her first book of poetry.

Author's note

un·ed·it·ed is a collection of poems from my heart. Each poem is a story, a facet, where you will find yourself inhabiting various roles; sometimes as a physician, a patient, a caregiver or simply an observer.

You will connect with the unedited raw vision these poems evoke in your soul. You will find yourself questioning the reasoning behind what you see and feel. In the end, I hope that you will emerge calm and accepting of the humanity a physician brings to your care.

Share your thoughts with me:
fakhanauthor@gmail.com